SOME POEMS FROM THE
COAST OF MAINE

Some Poems from the Coast of Maine

Mary Whitcomb Keep

A Keep Press Book

Copyright © 2013 Mary Whitcomb Keep

All rights reserved. For permission requests, write to the publisher at the address below.

Book design by Lisa von Schlegell
Cover design by Megan Futscher
Cover photo by Julia (von Schlegell) Hegan
Back cover photo by Rosemary von Schlegell

ISBN-10: 061581123X
ISBN-13: 978-0615811239

Keep Press
P.O. Box 1297
Ogunquit, ME 03907

DEDICATION

In memory of my brother Oliver Hoagland Keep

CONTENTS

Rue	1
Christmas Mass 1958	2
Meeting the Train 1929	3
With My Father in the Park	4
Beneath the Red Cliffs	6
The Little Fishes	7
The Sun Rising Like the Heart of God	8
At Dusk	9
Morning	10
The Star	11
Oh Dove	12
Lost Angel	13
This Grass, this River	14
Bracelet	15
Return from Berkeley	16
Angel I	18
My Cyclamen	19
Vernal Equinox	20
Child on a Winter Beach	21
April	22
The Donkey	23
The Summer Evening	24
The Nests	26
Meditations Prompted by Anna with Ollie	27
The Little One	28
Baby Creatures	30
Ode to Ollie	31
My Angel	32
The Birds	33

John Paul II in Boston September 1979	34
Waiting	35
Isaac	36
Death Is an Encounter	38
To Bruno/Phyllis	40
Goldenrod	41
Offering	42
Tony	43
Poet's Delight	44
Angel II	45
The Revelation	46
The Three Kings	47
The Coming of the Kings	48
The Return	50
The Coming of Spring	51
Snow in the Night	52
A Hopeful Equinoxial Spring Song	53
With Tony by Brenda's Pond	54
The Magnolia (To Nans and Tup)	55
Salted With Fire	56
Waked Before Morning	57
The Little Standing Stones	58
Reflection among these Rocks	60
In the Hearts of Stones	62
ABOUT THE AUTHOR	64

Rue

In all hours of twilight, in dreariest marshes
The sad poet, warily lurking, scarce daring to breathe,
Cold and despairful, watches for his prey,

And always, taken off guard, astonished out of a
    seeming sleep
And reaching to fight off, to hold for an instant in
    place, to embrace

The rushing and beating of those luminous forms

Finds in his trembling and irreverent hand
His punishment. For whoever will believe
Those tattered feathers grew on angels' wings?

n.d.

Christmas Mass 1958

In what simplicity and mercy He
Who continues holy comes to be
In us who by His grace
Absolved, here hold Him now as might
Some bleak and hideous place
Filled in the darkened night
By deep and unseen snows
Receive with still amaze and whole delight
The delicate embrace
And slow inflood of morning's first fresh rose.

n.d.

Meeting the Train 1929

About four in the morning we set forth in the Chevy
My beautiful mother and I,
A small child ignorant and trusting,
Carrying with us only a few pieces of plain bread.
I shall never forget the goodness of it
And the joy flooding my childish heart
As we rode together the seven miles to Wells station
Simple, rough and desolate, smelling of pine and
    cinders
Where we waited beside the hand car and the baggage
    scales
Looking anxiously down the track for what seemed
    hours
Until we heard the first faint far off whistle,
And through the scrub pine the black nosed engine
    suddenly appeared
Chugging and clanging, with its slowly lengthening
    line of cars,
And my dashing young father, impatient, jumped off
    into our world.

December 12, 1982

With My Father in the Park

Secure in the swing
For very little children
Whether it's up or down
I feel his arm
Behind me.

His arm holds me tight
On the merry-go-round
On my dapple grey,
And the music sounds
As we ride away,
And I take fright
And want to get off
But he whispers "stay."

He puts me into a tiny boat
The shape of a swan
And away I float,
And I think he's gone
'Till I find his face
In the crowd
And his smiling eyes
Upon me.

And he lifts me out

And carries me about
And sets me down
On the deep green lawn
And buys me corn
For the lamb and the fawn
That are just newborn.

It's time to go, and the amber glow
And the fading bell of the carousel
And the music of the band
Float down the darkening path to home;
Tired, I understand
And trot along beside him,
As he takes my hand.

April 1992

Beneath the Red Cliffs

When I was a child, maybe nine or ten
That age so firm and secure
Not yet quite tamed or tempered
We would stand there beneath the red cliffs,
Stalwart Dorothy with her red hair
And I – O valiant -
Two Vikings of the northern seas,
Confronting the high waves curling over themselves
In glorious, sunlit blue green tons of crushing power,
And just as they rose to demolish us,
Tumbling, crashing upon our fragile presumption,
We would dive – hurling ourselves with confident and
        joyous abandon, tunneling
Straight down to cool and peaceful depths beneath, to
        quietness, to dark green tombs
Still, deep and secure; Letting it all flow over us
Like thundering hooves; palatial jade hallways
        collapsing
In churning eddies of quivering and evanescent foam
    ...
And emerging beyond this destruction we would arise
With shouts of triumph – saved, jubilant and reborn!

December 6, 1982

The Little Fishes

I stand on these rocks at the turning tide
Where the sea meets the warm green river
Cold little currents that curl and slide
Creep up in swirls where the fishes hide
Where the fishes shy all shiver.

Not even those who wish to be wise
Nobody hears the little cries
The little hundred silver cries
Of the fish who vanish before your eyes
In the sand of the warm green river.

n.d.

The Sun Rising Like the Heart of God

No matter what the night,
That first rising with its stream of light
Over the water; molten the sun
Like a heart, like a valentine,
Clear, red gold, sweet and warm.

n.d.

At Dusk

It's growing dark and through the trees
The evening sky sprinkles its light
Like tiny stars.
The birds in pairs upon their nests
Sing evensong.

How beautiful this shadowed earth,
Ever changing ever fresh;
If lovely here so much we see
How radiant will heaven be.

August 2005

Morning

The trees are still and bare;
Now the sun is higher,
Silver in the air,
Silver in the water.

I care not for the noise,
The cares that will follow,
Here in this morning quiet,
Clear, free of sorrow.

n.d.

The Star

I started at dusk up the hill
To take in the wash,
And there was this star,
This big, clear planet hanging in the sky;
It was for me alone,
The first thing that day
Just for myself;
It was like You
Just for me
And yet just for anyone;
And I went down and told the others,
And they all went outside;
I don't know if they heard me.

n.d.

Oh Dove

Oh dove
You speak to me throughout the long day
In endless, faithful, identical
Yet ever fresh
Notes of sweetness and of love.

Oh doves
Through trials and distractions
You remain
Several
Yet somehow one
Like my soul's loves.

n.d.

Lost Angel

Lost Angel with your pale bright face turned down,
You may not speak, I may not even hear
The smallest rustle of your folded wings
Disturb the current of this heavy air,

Yet in the roots of sense that darkly lie insensible
I sometimes feel the gall,
Tender, relentless, perpetual,
Slow, hard drops of your bright tears that fall.

1948-1950

This Grass, this River

This grass, this river
That grass and those trees –
All are immediate and only present
This June afternoon.

Like this same and changing river
I feel time hang in the wind and shiver
Between its same and changing self
In the sun and shade
Of this June afternoon.

And coming home between the varied fields,
Some only buttercups, some daisies, flags or clover,
Or with red-orange Indian flares mixed all together
In the long, green, sweet grass, June yields
To a perpetual June as to a lover.

June 1955

Bracelet

I'm gonna make me a bracelet,
A bracelet of charms,
Of little white crosses
With the names of lost friends;

And wondering always
Just why they all fled
Count my sins and reproaches
On alternate days.

March 30-31, 1971

Return from Berkeley

Does it ever bother you about the animals?
She said on the way to the airport.
Sometimes the monkeys
The young man replied.

And as the plane rose
And the panorama of lights
Dazzled and, left behind,
Gave way to the hills,
Pockets and pinwheels of light,
Strange dark forms, glittering puzzles of maps,

Too late, too late to understand,
And we are beyond,
Tunneling through darkness
in this marvelous machine.

Conceived and fabricated by our own.

But what of the rabbits,
The little rats, the monkeys
And the dogs?
We have left them behind.
Their suffering is not our concern.
When they cry out "Where is God" we tell them
No one is watching.

There is no one who cares.
No one will come to save you
For there is no God,
Only the Advancement of Science,
That means the Satisfaction of Our Curiosity
And the Betterment of Our Condition
In this planet which We dominate.

Your sufferings are secondary.
We have all the priorities.
Look around
There is no one in charge but Us
There is no love
No contract of trust between us

There is no love
There is no trust
There is no God

And no one left to forgive us
When we cannot forgive ourselves.

March 1976

Angel I

Angel, you stay so far away
Respectfully;
Oh come a little closer, pray
With gentle wings encircle me
Perhaps just softly call;
For tho' you're with me night and day
You sojourn in eternity
And I am only human after all.

n.d.

My Cyclamen

Two young leaves on delicate long stems
Reach upward toward the light
Not the real sun – there isn't room -
Only the meager brightness of the lamp.
The leaves arrayed around choose each his place
From which to turn toward life;
Their yearning somehow breaks my heart;
There are no blossoms coming now;
I light the lamp each morning.

October 11-13, 2006

Vernal Equinox

Now where the winter wrung, the rainworm
        deliquescent snow has run
To meet the flood tides on the tumbled stones
Or swamped, recumbent, gently flailing grass, the
        mangled sand,
There melts and mingles, lies at ease and warm
The thin pale honey of an April sun,
Yet light as lies upon an old hand
The unasked kiss of a child.

And the heart now empty of innocence is stirred
By memory of loss like a transparent wind
Rising with notes of bird and waterfall
And aromatic of those primal flowers
Who waked like stars down fields of miracle
Where walked in cool and early violet hours
Dear and familiar feet, oh still unscarred.

April 1959

Child on a Winter Beach

She fords follows the sprung fresh seaward veins
All understained in the sandy wrist
By the bruised blue garnet traces
From their bright sliding
Down the biding inward faces of rock, or rising under
    the egg smooth innocent stones.
By the rocks where the barnacles lap and the barnacle
    bones
And blue and purple mussels cluster lustrous,
Are ingrained with wary crabs and drab snug faring
    snails
And the salt pools they cradle are green
Are full of miracle in the Easter of her eyes.
The boisterous gulls have flown
    have fled down the ribs of the tide.
Oh she has cried back the bitter beaked herring gulls
    and the tide
And flings the water willy-nilly tattered tails of weeds
    aside
And to the smoking dark blue ocean's open hand
Comes riding all the horses of the sand.

n.d.

April

*".... But the Springtime that I bring to souls by my grace –
These are what you should thank me for most of all."*
"He and I" – May 1, 1941

Whether it's rain or shine or even snow
Still it is April's snow, that's all I know;
The noisy dawn comes earlier each day,
The boisterous peepers sing
At evening, and there's peace
In knowing winter over and the spring
Advancing surely into summer's solstice.

The altar now bedecked with white and gold
The lilies heaped, the Pascal candle lit
The "Gloria" proclaimed to bells, the story told
In words familiar and divinely sweet,
The sudden burst of Alleluias sung
Tell Easter's joy accomplished and begun —
Christ risen, and for all our imperfection
We too – yes you and I –
Advancing daily into Resurrection.

April 10, 1986

The Donkey

Like the round head of a grieving child
Earth turns toward winter and the outcast sky,
All his blue streamers tattered and gone by,
And who shall pin on this small bulging donkey
A tale of spring to take upon his journey, so often
      turned,
'Till fragrant with lilac, with lily of the valley,
That heedless girl, green haired, blue eyed, shall pick
      him up,
Shall smile, shall kiss with a bright bit his mouth, his
      head adorning
With chains of stinging flowers and lead his way
Gently, through rains and down the unbound springs,
      and gay
In voices of birds waking with the day in her dark
      throat
Speak in his ear, while from uncertain meadows far
      away and near
The dove mourns early, Oh early now just where
Chill in white May, the short night turns toward
      morning.

n.d.

The Summer Evening

The summer evening softly lies;
The young, detached like butterflies
Cast in their time upon the skies,
Are leading their intenser lives.

Already an abundant crop
Of lilacs are faded and forgot;
Weigela and bridal wreath
And rhododendron bank the rock;

Wisteria white and weary hangs,
And lofty on its froth and fringe,
A catbird now the love song sings
My heart forgot in other springs.

Wings of the dying sky embrace,
Enflame the sea in blush of rose,
Melt with her sands, quiet her sighs
Beneath the first faint star's pure gaze.

The freshness of the salty air,
The rising fragrance of the earth
Mingle with the evening cries
Of children's play and nesting birds.

A soberer heaven inclines o'er all the land,
Watches, hesitates and lingers
Lightly with reluctant fingers;
Then his dark, mysterious hand.

n.d.

The Nests

When trees are stripped
the children come
      flailed
   cheeks aflame
   collecting nests
jackknife boys
girls with their unleavened breasts

Young knees grip
      bare
scaled trunk of pine
   lean birch
   with joy
 clamp upon
 bending switch
hands full of care
     reach
     prod
against short sun

Save for that
     odd
one who will not
 who'll watch
     burning
birch sun air
who will not
for the sake of the birds' returning.

Meditations Prompted by Anna with Ollie

She comes down early
Ollie on her shoulder
Sitting so proud
He flaps his cut wings
Hangs by his feet
Nestles up to her hair
Showing off like a child,
Squawks "Look at me".
His joy is full
As he sails along on her shirt.

I do not know how it can be,
The strangest thing it seems to me,
Spirits send birds to those they love,
Robin, oriole or dove,
Swallow, bluebird, bunting, sparrow;
Messengers of peace in sorrow.

Happiness, my father told me,
Is a bluebird, briefly, boldly
Lighting sudden on your shoulder.
Sadly though she will not stay,
Try to hold her
And she flies away.

n.d.

The Little One

There was a little star
And it wasn't very bright
And neither was it very big
Nor did it give much light,
In fact it was a dimmer star
Than many in the night.

Astronomers went looking for
The little stars one night,
The little weakly shining stars
That scarce spun into sight.
They thought to find the littlest
(It scarcely was a spark)
To name it just as Adam did
Before he pressed his luck,
And so they sought it east and west
To add it to their flock.

They found it hiding shyly
In a Magellanic cloud
And listed it "The Little One"
And called its name aloud.
Though I don't think it ever could
Light up the sky around
It shines oh much more brightly
Now it knows that it's been found.

March 10, 1998

Baby Creatures

Baby creatures, no matter who
Lion, wolf or Kangaroo
Elephant, monkey hippo too
So joyous, innocent and playful
Unlike their parents mean and hateful.

n.d.

Ode to Ollie

Ollie, if you don't quit that squawking
Even though you're so good looking
I'll really have to send you packing.
Tho' you're a universal wonder
And of you I'm ever fonder,
My poor ears you'll split asunder.
Ascended from a Pterodactyl,
How I love your gentle prattle;
Your little brain's a living fractal.
A microchip is not as small
And yet I think you're no one's fool;
In fact I think you know it all.
I love your cozy coo so sweet
And how you peck me on the cheek
When you appreciate a treat.
So wise that little mind, so smart,
So funny, loyal, bossy, sharp,
So full of love that tiny heart.

May 2000

My Angel

My Angel is always laughing,
Laughing with me, laughing at me
No matter how earnestly I try;
But it's all right considering
How often, long and bitterly
I've made him cry.

I said "Angel, didn't we write a terrific poem?
I really think it's a sensation."
He said "Oh well, you did the work,
I did the inspiration."

(Spin off)

May 27, 1998

The Birds

Sometimes, mostly to the innocent,
The firebird's inexplicable descent
From Paradise brings down a fiery dart
Of sudden joy to the astonished heart.

And then the little yellow bird that sings
Beneath the shadow of the raven's wings
Will leave our hearts, so weak and wayward, broken
Save for the quiet, gentle, soft, sweet token
Of the dove's mourning far and near,
Consoling, calling, always here.

Then too the owl, familiar, dark and somber
Scowls wisely perched on a reluctant shoulder
'Till comes the thrush, of all the throng the best;
Her lovely, looked for song she does not sing
But patient, pensive, stays upon her nest
That from her cloistered eggs new life may spring.

I sing down aisles of green
With light and shadow in between
The trees alive with birds
Seen and unseen.

May 1998

John Paul II in Boston September 1979

We were soaked in the rain
Pouring a blessing
We were filled with joy.
Everyone was running, laughing and crying.
Our eyes were streaming
Our tears falling on benches
       blankets, pavements and grass
It was like the second coming,
Priests, nuns, friars and us ordinary people
Diverse in color, culture and personality
All soaked to the skin on the Common
Up and down the avenues
Everyone smiling at each other
Out of our minds with joy.

It was 20 years ago this September.
I don't remember what you said,
A far off figure in white.
You've been so many places since,
And so much has happened to us all,
But never, never will I forget
The Love, the tears, the joy in the rain.

September 30, 1999 to May 28, 2000

Waiting

All day we waited for the snow to fall
From swollen clouds, and we could hardly bear
To think how it would churn the sullen air
And how the drifts would cling to the stone wall,
How it would crown the hill and deeply lie
Upon the quiet fields and clear the sky
And gently fill the barren maple tree
And foam, into that wicked pastel sea.

Now evening drains the quiet afternoon
No shadows form, it will not come we know,
Only the tarnished streaks of earlier snow
Still shame the naked land, and soon
Only the rising of a little wind
And the blue twilight sifting through the mind.

n.d.

Isaac

On the third day, leaving the rest, they walked
        together toward the distant hill,
He carrying the logs, his father only the flame
        flickering in the little vessel
And the knife sharpened for the sacrifice.
They rested toward midday only eating a bit of bread
With some light wine from the western vineyard;
A flock of doves flew up as they rose to go,
And all along the way he really knew.

His heart was stunned with the shadow that engulfed
        them
And overflowed with sorrow for the old man;
It puzzled him too, yet glancing at the face like stone
There was no sign of senility, only a sorrow he had
        never seen
Not even when Ishmael had gone.

He thought of his mother and prayed to be brave in the
        end
And seeing the fields and herds, the flocks and the
        brown brook,
The golden hills and little leaves dancing between light
        and shadow

He thought it hard to leave for paradise, but harder yet
    for those who'd stay behind,
And climbing the hill he reached for the worn familiar
    hand.

And then they stood there in the clearing
And his heart fainted as they laid the logs,
And he turned almost swooning to his father
And looked into the face he loved more than his life
And kissed and held and soothed the trembling hands.

July 2, 1981

Death Is an Encounter

Death is mysterious and horrifying,
Unnatural the separation of soul and body,
A violence, almost a tragedy -
No "almost" about it.

Yet death is Christmas morning.

Death is like the white owl we saw,
So strange, grotesque,
Turning his head right around
On a swivel
In a most unnatural way,
Looking at us with that
Inscrutable, catlike look
Like the sound "owl."

Death though is midnight mass with the snow falling.

Death is an encounter
No one can usurp;
No matter how difficult the journey,
Leaving cares and loves and all concern
For the cost of our funerals,
Light and blithe
We step in air,
Nor torturer

Nor benefactor
Can thwart us;

Like Simeon
We shall clasp Him,
Christ the King.

n.d.

To Bruno/Phyllis

These incandescent winter dawns
Awake in me the wintry hope
Passionless, of eternity.
No sun shall light that mystery
Not bound by time or place,
Yet brighter, better joy there reigns,
And we shall see Love's face.

March 10, 1999

Goldenrod

Goldenrod in sea wind
Against grey sand
So bright, so brave, so bold
At summer's end.
Oh let me too grow old
Like you my stalwart friend
Before blue sky to stand
And bend
Laden with gold
As the winds grow cold.

September 21-25, 1995

Offering

The wound offered
Cannot fester
Like a flower
Unfurls
Gives fragrance
In the sun

Pain
Like talent
Love, remorse, joy
Whatever its degree
Buried grows rank
Misered is devalued

Given to God
Remains innocent
Grows strong
Grows sweet
Bears fruit

n.d.

Tony

As you my child are the limitation
So are you the sweetest consolation of my life
And imitation of our Lord.

Clearer than all in my heart
Your hands marked with the strange line
Raised, raise my compassion
Cling around my heart.

Oh beautiful calm face
So small, so quiet beside me
You have kept me from destruction.
Oh how can we ever fathom

The strange economy of a loving God;
Why does our trust so often fail
With salvation springing even here along our path.

n.d.

Poet's Delight

Through these green and lonesome days
With little children still to raise
And anxious for our daily bread
"Your life is over", someone said
Composing my sad epitaph….
I look at the full page of praise
And laugh.

n.d.

Angel II

Angel! When I finally accepted
The fact of your presence
And even that it might have been
You who produced those poems
I just had assumed were "mine",
I admit I did feel rather put out
Not to say fairly "put down",
But now Angel, most dear,
I would like to ask today
Are you still there?
Do you care?
Have you in fact anything more to say?

February 18, 1988

The Revelation

He was revealed to the Angels
To his mother and Joseph
And to John and Elizabeth
And finally Zachary,
Then to the shepherds and their families
And trusted friends,
To the three Kings and their retinues
And later all their families
And to Simeon and Anna too;
And were there some at Herod's court
Who understood?

It seems like God could hardly wait
To tell the secret, and He had hardly come
To reason when He sent Him to His temple
To reveal Himself to those whose hearts were pure
And ready to receive his coming.
Yes, surely the revelation came to some -
Perhaps to some who couldn't wait
Those eighteen years of his obedience -
A knowledge more sudden and astounding,
More precious, sweet and awesome than any they had
      ever known.

January 22, 1992

The Three Kings

They were wealthy, wise and royal;
They knew the stars and men,
History, trade and war,
Farming, mining, music and literature
And how to rule;
They knew between them much
And surmised even more.

They knew suffering, disillusionment and joy
And they came with hearts like children's,
Pure, full of wonder and amazement
Melting like wax within them,
While fear and trembling overtook them
As never before.

Arriving at night
They pitched their tents in the open field
And walked together in silence
Beneath the incredible star,

Caspar, philosophical old warrior,
Balthazar, supple and wary as a panther,
And shrewd, impassive Melchior.

January 1992

The Coming of the Kings

Of course they found a house in Bethlehem
Or half a house or an upstairs apartment
Perhaps with a sunny rooftop where the baby played -
And always that star at night that seemed to mark them
And then one evening, late, with that marvelous star overhead
The clanking and jingling of bells and pots and harnesses,
Camels snorting, dogs barking and a whole retinue by the little house,
And the three personages – foreign, unique, mysterious,
Slowly approaching in silence, speaking low at the entrance,
Falling upon their faces prostrate before the child
Tears streaming down their leathered cheeks, unable to rise -
The end and beginning of their journey;

Then the gifts humbly brought forth, significant and strange,
Prophetic, wildly extravagant to the little household -
These men had the bearing of kings and were so in their far off lands.

She handed them the child; each in turn held him in his
    arms
And looked and looked and smiled – and he smiled
    and touched the fur
Around Caspar's neck and the tassels on Melchior's
    hood
And fell asleep in the blue black arms of Balthazar.

And they talked softly to his mother and Joseph
And they stayed in the town until the warning came
And brought camels' milk and honey, strange shaped
    rolls
Nectar and fruits, bells, coats of camels' hair
Blankets and a wooden doll and toys
Returning over and over to worship him. And they
    prayed,
Prayed for him and his family, for each other, for their
    nations
And the world, for the past and the future to be
    redeemed
And finally left one night after saying a last goodbye
Slipping quietly eastward by a different way.

January 11, 1992

The Return

Oh what a Passover it was
When the Angel called them out of Egypt,
When the Lord God almighty
Retraced the steps of His ancestors,
Sitting upon the donkey, running before His mother.

How old was He? How tall?
Did they mingle with a caravan?
Did He get to ride a camel,
Climb the gnarled olive trees,
Chase the little vipers under their rocks
And pick for Mary all the desert flowers?

Did he speak their dialects a bit
Playing with little Arab boys
And plunge in ferny pools in desert heat?
Did they sing songs as they travelled along
And did Joseph teach Him along the way?

And did He stand where Moses stood
With the mystery of His mission in His eyes
And survey the land, twice blessed,
He had given to his people?

November 27, 1991

The Coming of Spring

Like the round head of a grieving child
Earth turns toward winter and the outcast sky,
All his blue streamers tattered and gone by,
And who shall pin on this small bulging donkey
A tale of spring to take upon his journey
So often turned, 'till fragrant with Lilac and Lily of the
      Valley
That heedless girl, green haired blue eyed
Shall pick him up, shall smile,
Shall kiss with a bright bit his mouth
His head adorning with chains of stinging flowers
And lead his way gently through rains and down the
      unbound springs.
And gay with voices of birds waking with the day
In her dark throat, speak in his ear
While from uncertain meadows far away and near
The dove mourns early, oh early now just where
Chill in white May, the short night turns toward
      morning.

n.d.

Snow in the Night

Snow is silent as it falls,
Winds howl, the ocean roars,
And miles out the sea bell tolls
Its penetrating warning in my ears.

Boards creak, boughs crack.
I hear the rumble of the welcome plough.
Pumpkin, my golden cat comes back
From chilling dark adventures all aglow.

Snow falls softly without a sound,
Gently invasive and secret as the gift of prayer,
And in the morning light the world around
Is bent and bowed in peace
As deep, as white, as pure
As the lamb's soft fleece.

March 2001

A Hopeful Equinoxial Spring Song

Oh what a verdant spring we'll have this year
With snow upon snow, now no longer fair,
Flooding the frozen earth beneath the sun
Who day by day now surely shall return.

The mourning dove shall gently raise her voice,
The chickadee and robin come again,
The cardinal and his mate make us rejoice
With the small finch, the hummingbird and wren.

Nests shall be built where hungry young can grow,
While fragrant breezes through our houses flow,
And sun and rain melt tarnished snow away
And coax from buried bulbs a spring bouquet.

March 2001

With Tony by Brenda's Pond

Their voices cut the stillness down the empty road,
A clearing opens and a snowy pond
Fringed with the blackness of the winter pines,
The childish figures in the luminous glow
Of winter sunshine sliding to and fro,
The quiet blue grey sky that overhangs
This now familiar winterscape swung round
Year after year; the pale memories crowd,
Leave in the heart the soft ash of despair....

The growth of love, stunted and stunned and cored,
Friendships soured by spite, choked by the waves
Of envy, anger and the unkind word,
My fathers lying in their unseen graves,
Fertility and flowering never to be attained,
The teasing of talents, directions,
Deep commitments out of reach....

I look down to the little hand I hold
Of this almost futureless child,
The little steps eager along the road;
His name is Love,
This innocent talisman given to me by God.

n.d.

The Magnolia
(To Nans and Tup)

My bare magnolia tree so quiet stands
Daring the wind and snow and freezing rains;
So delicate her grace, yet she retains
Like hope her perfect little buds along each branch.

So early in the northern spring, a rarity
These tiny globes so proud and prim
Like pale pink lamps set out to trim
'Till under his benign authority

She throws discretion to the ascending sun
And uncurls every folded one
Patterned against the deep May skies
Like stars or lovely butterflies.

Sweet tree transplanted from the south,
Like a bright bride you issue forth;
Your virginal blooms announce our spring,
Fulfilled in their surrendering.

May 11, 1985

Salted With Fire

It's worth growing old I do believe
For the ongoing instruction that we receive.
In spite of our aches and pains and sorrows
We see the past and the tomorrows
Understood with a new clarity:
Our ingratitude for love and charity,
The wounds we heedlessly inflicted,
The paths we chose, the paths rejected;
Taunted by demons until we tire
We are salted with purgatorial fire,
And though to our fancy it doesn't cater
It's better to bear it now than later!

August 23, 2000

Waked Before Morning

Waked before morning
The tender heart's a child
Stayed in too long
For all his mother's warning.

His lips are purple, tremble
His eyes are starred with salt
He chatters one word like an idiot.

Flung on a warm rock
As in a cradle wild
Swung from a treetop, rocked
Seasick, he hears the bough crack

And the heart turns over
As leaves before a storm
Turning their pale sides out show the dark veins
And all the ferns' bright eyes, and learns
How nay returns
As the wave returns
As the dark turns with the day

Until the round tide tugging at the stones
Dulls, roars him to edge of sleep
Where reaching down he feels
The gold sun in the grey rock take his bones.

The Little Standing Stones

As I walk before sunrise on this lovely path
Quiet in the grey mists, looking seaward always,
I am amazed to see that someone
Children perhaps, prophet or idiot,
Has turned the rocky coves to miniature
And charming Easter Islands
With little piles of carefully stacked stones that crowd
Like a vast throng mutely gazing seaward,
While others, lonely sentinels, crown crumbling
       basaltic rocks
Or a dark flow of lava or some smooth granite boulder
Or lurk in twos or threes in sandy corners.

And all along my path in every cove they stand
Primitive, attentive, somehow oriental,
Quaint and mysterious,
Silently commemorating or awaiting what?
Some marvelous event or prophecy's fulfillment,
Some seminal invasion, longed for reunion
Or anticipated, wondrous, joyful welcoming?

The dawn spreads over the grey seas,
The sun bursts suddenly red
Out of the far horizon
'Till it breaks away and rides

Exultant, molten, free
Swift and ever climbing in the opening sky.

And they remain, touching, grey and silent
Mysterious monuments, yearning heralds, patient
        witnesses
Who stand before the annihilating flood
Awaiting the moment of their visitation.
My heart exalted, awed
Hot beating in the salty freshness of the air
Bursts from its shackles, innocent and bare,
And takes its place among them joined to theirs.

n.d.

Reflection among these Rocks

Crumbs of an ancient catastrophe, this far, flayed
Figurescape of rocks is jumbled.
Flat gleam by night graveyards of snails
Sundrained, rimewhite among the shambles.

The oiled flanks lie solid to the sky.

One high tide island rises high,
Old, furred with sparse grass,
Dead white with guano from its circling gulls –
Crow Island, and it's true they come
Side by side sometimes, the ragged fierce
Crows with the fierce furled gulls, black and white,
      unenlightened
Kings of their mangy castle standing arrayed
In dignity by the rainpools of slime

Thrice seldom hurricane sweetened.

And the dark masses are darkened.
Only a thin crest traces far away
Its death among stones, where new awakened
The silent, light encrusted crescent cape rejoices
Cradling the children of the roiled bay,

And heaven like a cowled monk recollected, counts
    silver rosaries,

When through these miniature canals and weedy
    waterways,
Out from among the rocks and watery voices,
A white ship dips and sails, her hull of nacre; or albino
    gull;
Or wandering white horse grazes the drenched new
    meadows
Far from the warm barns, the isles of myth;
A pure spirit, a pool of light among the pools,
An angel moves – oh lambent now the shadows –

The rising moon now traveling the earth.

n.d.

In the Hearts of Stones

In the hearts of stones
And rivers, eyes of lime
Pools of amber
In small blue eggs in the nest
And sun and shade on the grass
Your hand
And the wide cool floor of the mind
I found calm.

In many times and places
Calm lies buried, ready to emerge
At our touch and burst our hearts with joy.

If only we could carry
Into the frightened, angry, foolish wastes of time
Something equivalent, something to lead us back
To the hearts of stones and rivers
Lime green pools and eyes of amber
To the small blue eggs in the nest
Sun and shade on the grass
The hand of whom we love
And the rock cool floor of the mind.

n.d.

ABOUT THE AUTHOR

Mary Whitcomb Keep was born in New Jersey in 1926 to Oliver Davis and Helen Raymond (Whitcomb) Keep. She spent summers in Ogunquit, Maine as a child, and has lived on the coast since her early 20s. She was married to the sculptor David von Schlegell and has three grown daughters and a son with Down's syndrome. Brought up an Episcopalian, she became a Catholic in 1962.

She has always written poetry.

Mary lives with her son Anthony near the Marginal Way and Little Beaches of Ogunquit, in the house she summered in with her parents as a child.

www.ingramcontent.com/pod-product-compliance
Lightning Source LLC
Chambersburg PA
CBHW071744040426
42446CB00012B/2471